BRIDGES

Chris Oxlade

Belitha Press

First published in Great Britain in 1996 by
 Belitha Press Limited
London House, Great Eastern Wharf
Parkgate Road, London SW11 4NQ

Reprinted in 1998

Designers: Steve Wilson and Maria D'Orsi
Series Designer: Hayley Cove
Editor: Christine Hatt
Illustrator: Martin Woodward
Picture researcher: Diana Morris
Consultant: Conor Murphy

ISBN 1 85561 511 8

Printed in Spain

British Library Cataloguing in Publication Data
CIP data for this book is available from the British Library.

Photographic credits
J. Allan Cash Ltd: 11, 13, 19, 25.
Collections/Brian Shuel: 10
Military Picture Library: 35
Zefa: 14

The publishers would also like to thank Sheilagh Chadfield of Cleveland Structural
Engineering Limited for her help throughout the project.

Words in **bold** appear in the glossary on page 46.

Contents

Bridges

At some time during most car and train journeys we cross over or go under a bridge. Bridges carry vehicles and people quickly and easily over obstacles such as rivers, valleys, roads and railways. They are an important part of a country's transport system. Bridges over rivers make a slow ferry journey or a long **detour** unnecessary. Bridges over valleys mean that motorways and railways do not have to be built up and down steep slopes. Bridges over roads and railways mean that cars and trains do not have to stop to let other vehicles pass.

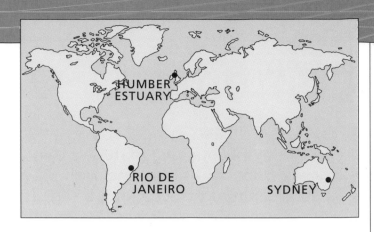

Rio-Niteroi Bridge Factfile
Structure: Box girder beam
Overall length: 13.9 km
Central span: 300m
Height in middle: 63m
Completed: 1974
Architect: Redpath Dorman Long/Cleveland Bridge and Engineering Co.

The vast Rio-Niteroi Bridge carries a road between Rio de Janeiro and Niteroi in Brazil. It is the longest beam bridge in the world.

The Humber Bridge is a suspension bridge over the Humber Estuary in the north of England. In 1995, it was still the longest bridge in the world.

What sort of bridge?

You have probably seen many different sizes and shapes of bridge, but there are really only three types: beam bridges, arch bridges and suspension bridges. Before they can decide which type of bridge to build, architects and engineers must find out the **span** (the distance the bridge must cover without a support), the shape of the surrounding land, and whether the bridge has to cross water. They must also think about the traffic that will use the bridge, and how much space is needed for ships, trains or lorries to pass underneath.

Past, present and future

The Romans were the first serious bridge-builders. They constructed a huge network of roads and bridges throughout their empire. The only building materials they had were wood and stone, and with these they could only construct a long bridge by building a row of short arches side by side. Arch bridges remained the main type of bridge until the eighteenth century, when iron was first used in bridge-building. With iron, builders could construct beam and suspension bridges. Almost all modern bridges are built of steel and concrete. These materials, and better construction techniques, allow longer bridges than ever before to be built. Small bridges can be constructed more quickly, too.

▼ **Sydney Harbour Bridge Factfile**

Structure:	Steel arch
Length of arch:	503m
Height in middle:	52m
Width of roadway:	49m
Completed:	1932
Architect:	Redpath Dorman Long

Humber Bridge Factfile ▼

Structure:	Steel deck suspended under steel cables
Overall length:	2220m
Central span:	1410m
Height in middle:	30m
Height of towers:	162.5m
Completed:	1981
Architect:	Freeman Fox and Partners

The Sydney Harbour Bridge in Sydney, Australia, carries both road and railway traffic and is the widest bridge in the world.

STEP BY STEP

In this space on each double page we show you a stage in the building of an imaginary beam bridge. The sequence starts here and ends on page 21.

1 Before bridge-building can start, geologists must survey the site. They test the ground by drilling **boreholes** with a rig.

Beam bridges

A beam bridge is made of one or more beams – long pieces of wood, concrete, or other building material – supported at each end. Beam bridges can be as simple as a log laid over a stream, or as complex as a long road bridge with several beams and supports made from concrete and steel. Here and on the following eight pages, you can find out how beam bridges work and the different methods and materials that are used to build them.

A single span beam bridge is supported at either end, but has no piers in the middle.

SHORT SINGLE SPAN

A multiple span beam bridge is supported at the ends and by piers between spans.

THREE SEPARATE SPANS

A continuous span beam bridge is supported both at the ends and by piers in the middle.

LONG SINGLE SPAN

The weight of traffic causes compression and tension in beams.

WEIGHT
COMPRESSION
TENSION

How a beam bridge works

The forces on a bridge are called loads. Live load is the weight of the traffic, dead load is the weight of the bridge and wind load is the force of the wind. When there is live load on a beam, the beam bends down. As it bends, the material in the top of the beam is squashed (this is called **compression**), and the material in the bottom is stretched (this is called **tension**). If it bends too much, the beam collapses.

Parts of a beam bridge

Many beam bridges have one central span and two side spans. Each span is made up of several concrete beams, and the **road deck** is laid on the top. The beams are supported by **piers** and **abutments**, which rest on solid underground **foundations**.

Beam bridges are the most common bridge type and often carry a minor road over a motorway. This one has a central span and two side spans.

ABUTMENT
CONCRETE BEAMS SUPPORT ROAD DECK
CENTRAL SPAN
ROAD DECK MADE FROM SLAB OF CONCRETE
SIDE SPAN
PIER

Expanding and contracting

Most materials expand (grow longer) as the temperature rises, and contract (grow shorter) as it falls. Bridge beams behave like this as the weather changes from hot to cold. They also bend slightly as traffic crosses over them. If the ends of beams were fixed in place, this expanding, contracting and bending would make them crack. So beams rest on special sliding pads called bearing plates, which allow them to move slightly. The road deck also has expansion joints in it, which allow parts of the deck to expand and then contract without cracking.

Expansion joints are made of layers of rubber folded in a concertina shape between steel plates.

RUBBER LAYERS

STEEL PLATES

EXPANSION JOINT

BEARING PLATE

RUBBER PADS

I beam

M beam

STEEL PLATES

BOLT HOLES

Bearing plates consist of rubber pads between steel plates that are bolted firmly into position.

Beam shapes

The shape of a beam is designed to prevent it from bending too much, and to keep it as lightweight as possible. The more vehicles a beam has to support and the longer it is, the deeper and heavier it also needs to be. It is impossible to build extremely long beam bridges because the beams would have to be so thick that they would collapse under their own weight.

One common type of steel beam is called an I beam. Its cross-section (seen by looking at the beam from the end) makes it very strong for its weight. Concrete M beams are also widely used.

STEP BY STEP

2 Watertight **cofferdams** are built in the river bed. These keep the water out while engineers build the bridge's pile foundations.

Firm foundations

Hidden in the ground under every bridge is one of its most important parts – the foundations. The foundations support the weight of the bridge and the traffic on it, carrying it down into solid ground. If there were no foundations, the bridge supports would probably sink, making the bridge collapse. Piers and abutments support the beams in a beam bridge. In turn, the underground foundations support the piers and abutments.

Choosing foundations

There are several different types of foundation. The type chosen for a bridge depends on the weight each bridge pier will have to carry and the **geology** – the type of soil and rock – of the ground. A geological survey is always carried out before the bridge is built. It may reveal an area of solid rock, layers of different types of rock, or deep, soft soil.

*Bridge piers need to be supported by solid **bedrock**. If this is not just below the ground, engineers sink piles to reach it.*

Rock solid

The firmest foundations rest on solid rock. If there is solid rock near the surface, the base for a pier can be built directly on top of it. If the solid rock is deeper down, buried under layers of soil, long steel or concrete columns, called **piles**, are sunk instead. They reach right down to the solid rock, and the piers rest on top of them.

Concrete rafts

Where the soil underneath a bridge pier is deep and soft, special foundations are needed to spread out the bridge's weight so that the ground does not sag under it. One way of doing this is to build a massive concrete slab, called a **raft**. This allows the bridge to 'float' on top of the soil.

Concrete rafts are used to support bridge piers when solid rock is far below the ground and cannot be easily reached by piles.

8

Building in shallow water

Beam bridges can be constructed across areas of shallow water by building a series of piers in the water. First, the water must be temporarily moved aside to excavate and build the foundations. In very shallow water, a cofferdam is built around the site of the foundation, and the water is pumped out.

A cofferdam is made by driving interlocking steel plates into the river bed.

COFFERDAM

FLOATING CRANE

INTERLOCKING STEEL PLATES

Building in deep water

In deeper water, a structure called a caisson is used. A caisson is a huge concrete or steel tube that reaches from the surface down to the riverbed. **Silt** from the riverbed is dug out by cranes, or by workers inside a pressurized compartment in the bottom of the caisson. When the caisson is finally resting on solid rock, it is weighted down with **ballast**, such as concrete, to keep it in place. It then forms a solid base for the piers.

Open-ended caissons are built directly on to solid bedrock underneath deep water.

CRANE

SHARP EDGES

FLOATING DREDGER

CAISSON

*1 The sharp edges of the caisson help it to sink as a crane on a **dredger** digs silt from the river.*

BASE FOR PIER

CONCRETE BALLAST

2 Once in place, the caisson is weighted down with ballast and a pier base is built on top.

STEP BY STEP

3 Massive pre-stressed concrete beams for the bridge are manufactured in a factory and later transported to the site.

Concrete beams

Concrete is the material most commonly used for bridge-building. It is made by mixing small stones, cement and water. The mixture gradually sets, producing a very hard, long-lasting material. To make beams, fresh concrete is poured into moulds, then left to set. Concrete is also used to build other parts of a bridge, such as the foundations, the piers and the road deck. It is usually strengthened with steel bars rather than used on its own.

This typical concrete beam bridge spans a section of the M25, the motorway that surrounds London.

Reinforced concrete

Concrete is extremely difficult to squash (it is strong in compression), but easier to pull apart (it is weak in tension). On its own, it would be useless for making beams, which are both squashed and pulled by loads. To make beams stronger, steel bars are added where the concrete would be in tension. This combination of concrete and steel is called reinforced concrete. The steel in most bridge beams is stretched, either before the concrete sets (pre-stressing), or after it sets (post-stressing). This makes a beam even stronger.

PRE-STRESSING CONCRETE

*1 First, a steel bar is pulled from both ends until taut. This process is called **tensioning**.*

2 Next the tensioned bar is placed inside a wooden mould, and concrete poured over it.

3 Once the concrete is set, the steel is released and the wooden mould removed.

POST-STRESSING CONCRETE

1 Concrete is poured into a mould containing a hollow tube, then left to set.

2 The mould is removed, then a steel bar is threaded through the tube and tensioned.

3 A grip is attached to the steel bar to keep it tensioned. This process is called tying off.

STEEL BARS

CONCRETE

This cross-section of a concrete beam shows the position of the reinforcing steel bars.

Pre-cast concrete

Pre-cast concrete is moulded in a factory away from the building site. Many bridges are built with standard-sized, pre-cast beams. For other bridges, pre-cast beams have to be specially made. The standard-sized beams are much cheaper. Pre-cast beams are normally pre-stressed, too.

ROAD DECK

I-BEAMS

STEEL BARS HOLD BOXES TOGETHER

BOX BEAMS

ROAD DECK

Pre-cast concrete I beams or box beams are often used to build road decks. The beams are placed side by side and the deck is built in-situ on the top.

*A complex wooden framework like this is called **formwork**. It acts as a mould for in-situ concrete.*

In-situ concrete

Concrete made at a building site is called **in-situ concrete**. This is used to construct the road deck, piers and abutments and to strengthen the pre-cast beams. Very large or complicated beams are normally also made in-situ, as they would be difficult to transport from a factory.

VOIDS

REINFORCED CONCRETE

A road deck can also be built using a voided slab. This is a type of concrete beam and deck combined that contains tube-shaped voids (holes). These make the slabs lighter without losing much of their strength.

STEP BY STEP

4 Concrete piers for the new bridge are built on top of the pile foundations that have been driven deep into the river bed.

Girders and trusses

Most short bridges are made with simple concrete beams, but there are other ways of making beams and using them to build bridges. On these two pages you can see several of the most common. Some may look complicated, but they still work in the same way as simple concrete beams.

Steel girders

Steel plate girders are similar to concrete beams, but they are made by **welding** or bolting together flat sheets of steel. Plate girders are sometimes used instead of concrete beams, but in the same way. They are placed side by side and a concrete road deck is moulded on top. Plate girders are often used to build short railway bridges.

Building a plate girder railway bridge. The two large girders will form the basic structure of the bridge. Smaller girders resting between them will support the track.

Trusses

A **truss** is a beam made by joining lengths of steel called **struts** and **ties** to form a framework. Trusses are more complicated to build than plate girders, but they are much lighter, and use less steel. Truss bridges normally consist of two trusses, with the deck supported between them. Today, trusses are more often used for small, temporary bridges than for large, permanent ones. This is because they are easy to transport in small pieces, and relatively simple to construct on site.

Close-up of a plate girder

PLATE GIRDERS

REINFORCED CONCRETE PIERS

TIE STRUT

In a truss (left), the struts and ties are held together at the ends with bolts. The triangular shapes formed by the struts and ties keep the whole truss in shape.

This truss railway bridge carries trains over the Ogun River near Ibadan in western Nigeria.

A cross-section of a box girder (right). The shape is like two beams placed side by side.

BOX GIRDER

Concrete box girder sections are joined by threading thick steel wires through holes, then tightening them up.

STEEL WIRES

JOINED BOX GIRDER SECTIONS MAKE BEAM

Box girders

A **box girder** is a beam with a cross-section in the shape of a box. This shape makes it very stiff and strong. Box girders are normally used for long beam bridges, and are large enough to carry a road or railway on top. They can be made from thin steel plates that are welded together, or from moulded concrete. Box girders are normally made in short sections in a factory, then joined together later to make a box girder bridge. A concrete road deck is laid over the joined girder sections.

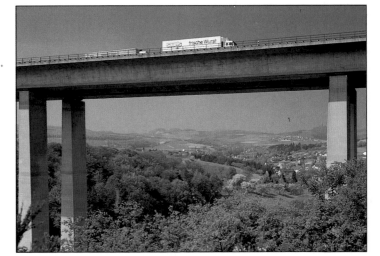

This concrete box girder bridge carries a motorway over a valley.

STEP BY STEP

5 Massive concrete abutments are built on both the river banks to provide strong support for the bridge beams.

Cantilever bridges

A cantilever is a beam supported at only one end. The other end hangs freely in mid-air. A simple cantilever bridge has two cantilever arms reaching into the centre from piers at the sides. The cantilever arms do not topple over because the abutments at the ends of the bridge hold them down. Like other types of beam, cantilevers can be made from concrete, steel or both.

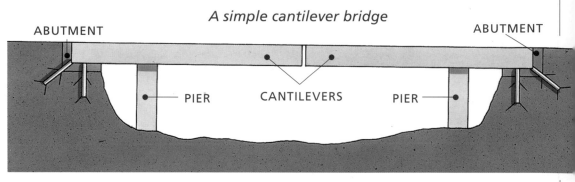

A simple cantilever bridge

ABUTMENT · PIER · CANTILEVERS · PIER · ABUTMENT

Suspended spans

Sometimes cantilevers on their own cannot make a long enough bridge. One way of making a cantilever bridge longer is to add a short beam between the ends of the two cantilever arms. A beam of this type is called a suspended span because it hangs between the cantilever arms without touching the bridge's sides.

Balanced cantilevers

Cantilevers do not have to be held down at both ends of a bridge. One cantilever arm can be balanced by another on the opposite side of a pier. This arrangement is called a balanced cantilever. A long bridge can be built by placing several balanced cantilevers end to end. It can be made even longer by adding suspended spans between each of the balanced cantilevers.

The Forth Railway Bridge in Scotland has a central balanced cantilever and two suspended spans. The cantilever arms are truss girders made by joining sections of thick steel tubing.

A suspended span cantilever bridge

CANTILEVER

SUSPENDED SPAN

Building cantilevers

Many modern cantilever bridges have arms made from pre-cast concrete or steel sections. The foundations and piers of the bridges are built first. Then the cantilever arms are built out from the piers.

Perfect balance

The cantilevers are built in each direction at the same rate. The pier does not tip over because the arms always balance each other perfectly. Finally, the arms are joined with a small section called the **key**.

BUILDING A BALANCED CANTILEVER

A concrete balanced cantilever bridge is built in several stages.

1 First, the foundations, piers and abutments of the bridge are constructed.

4 The cantilevers on one side are extended to the abutment and new cantilevers are then built out from the second pier.

2 Next, cantilever arms are built out from both sides of one of the piers.

5 Finally, the key segment is added in the centre, to complete the bridge.

3 The sections are joined together by tightened steel wires called tendons.

STEP BY STEP

6 The concrete side beams are lifted into place by huge cranes working from the river banks. Slowly, the bridge is taking shape.

Arch bridges

Arches are very simple structures that can be built from **masonry** (stone, brick or concrete) alone, without any steel reinforcement. For this reason they are one of the oldest types of bridge. (The other is the simple stone beam.) Arch bridges may have existed more than 5000 years ago. Few arch bridges are built today, because it is much easier and cheaper for engineers to construct cantilever or cable-stayed bridges.

Any weight on an arch bridge travels down its vertical supports, along the curve of the arch to the abutments, and down into the ground.

WEIGHT TRAVELS DOWN SUPPORTS

ROAD DECK

ARCH

FORCE ON ABUTMENTS

How an arch bridge works

You can think of an arch as a beam bent down at the ends. Weight on top of the arch is carried down to the ends and into the ground. The shape of the arch means that a load causes compression but not tension in it. This makes it possible to build an arch from masonry, which is strong in compression, but weak in tension. Any weight pushes down and out at the ends of the arch. Heavy abutments are needed to stop the arch from spreading outwards.

The Hell Gate Bridge, which carries rail traffic over East River in New York, USA, was completed in 1916. The steel used in this massive arch weighs 39 200 tonnes.

Swiss engineer Robert Maillart designed the 1930 Salginatobel Bridge, a concrete arch in the Alps.

HANGERS

SUPPORTS

Three different types of spandrel arch. The road deck can run over (left), under (centre), or through (right) the arch.

Modern arches

Most modern arch bridges are made from concrete or a steel frame. Concrete arches normally have the road deck resting on the top, supported by vertical columns. Steel frame arches are made by joining lengths of steel, in the same way as truss girders. Until suspension bridges were developed, the bridges with the longest spans were steel arches. Arch bridges can have a longer span than beam or cantilever bridges, but are more difficult to build.

Arch bridge designs

There are several different designs of arch bridge. Old arch bridges are called solid arches because the gap between the arch and the deck is filled. A spandrel arch has a separate arch and deck, connected by **hangers** and vertical supports. The road deck can hang underneath the arch, go through the arch, or sit over the arch.

Building a concrete arch

Concrete arches are normally made with in-situ concrete and built from the outside into the middle. The piers at the ends of the arch are built first, then used to support the moulds, called formwork, in which the concrete is left to set. Sometimes the central part of the arch is made on the ground and added in one huge piece, to complete the curved shape.

BUILDING A CONCRETE ARCH BRIDGE

1 The abutments in the valley sides and the two piers at either end of the bridge are built first.

2 Next, the formwork is hung on the piers and the arch is made using in-situ concrete.

*3 The centre section of the concrete arch is made on the ground and lifted into place with **winches**.*

4 The concrete road deck, side beams and more piers are added to complete the new bridge.

STEP BY STEP

7 Once the side beams are securely in place, the road deck can be added over them. It is constructed using in-situ concrete.

Suspension bridges

The bridges with the longest spans in the world are all suspension bridges. In a suspension bridge, the deck hangs from long cables. Spans of over 1 km are quite common, and a bridge with a central span of almost 2 km is due to open in Japan in 1998. There is no reason why longer spans should not be built. A bridge over 3 km long between Italy and Sicily is already planned. Suspension bridges are used to cross wide, deep rivers, or even seas.

How a supension bridge works

A suspension bridge has four main parts. These are the towers (sometimes called pylons), cables, hangers (sometimes called suspenders) and deck. The weight of the vehicles travelling over the road deck of a suspension bridge pulls down on the cables, trying to stretch them. In turn, the cables pull down and sideways on the towers. But the towers do not topple inwards because the cables are fixed to extremely strong **anchors** on the bank.

Suspension bridge cables are made of thousands of strands of steel wire bundled together. The strands are protected by a metal sheath around the cable. A single cable may be over 1m thick.

STRANDS OF STEEL WIRE

METAL SHEATH

TOWERS MADE OF HOLLOW CONCRETE OR STEEL

ANCHOR

The ends of the bridge cables are fixed into anchors. Where possible, the anchors are set in solid rock on the river bank. Where there is no rock, massive slabs of concrete, often as big as blocks of flats, are built instead.

CABLE

ANCHOR BOLT

The weight of a suspension bridge and its traffic load pulls down on the bridge cables. The cables pull on the towers. But these do not fall down because anchors hold the cables in position.

CABLES PULL ON TOWERS

WEIGHT OF ROAD AND TRAFFIC PULLS ON CABLES AND HANGERS

CABLES PRESS DOWN ON TOWERS AND FOUNDATIONS

CABLES PULL ON ANCHORS

The deck is made of steel sections supported by hangers on each side. This design makes it stiff, and stops it swaying in the wind.

HANGERS

STEEL SECTIONS

BOLTS

CLAMP

HANGER CABLE

Like the cables, the hangers are made of steel wires. At the top of each one is a large clamp that grips the cable firmly.

TOWER

CABLES

ROAD DECK

HANGERS

ANCHOR

Simple suspensions

This simple rope suspension bridge crosses the River Mahaweli in Kandy, Sri Lanka.

Not all suspension bridges are complicated concrete and steel structures. In many parts of the world, simple suspension bridges carry paths over rivers. The cables, which can be made of either thick rope or steel, form part of the walkway.

This diagram of a suspension bridge highlights its essential parts – cables, towers, hangers and deck. The anchors in the river bank are also essential. Without them, the bridge would collapse.

STEP BY STEP

8 Once the road deck covers the side beams, the central span beams are lifted up from a barge in the river by cranes.

Building a suspension bridge

The construction of a large suspension bridge is a major civil engineering project. Suspension bridges are normally built over water, and the building site can be several kilometres long. This makes construction more difficult than on land. Foundations and piers usually have to be built in water, and workers and building materials have to be carefully organized.

Deciding where to build

Choosing the right place to build a suspension bridge is vital. It is not always possible to build the bridge in the most convenient place for traffic. The river may be so wide or deep there that the bridge would be too expensive to construct, or the type of ground there may make it difficult to build solid foundations. It is often cheaper and easier to move further along the river, then build new roads to reach the ends of the bridge.

Many suspension bridges have steel towers. These are made in sections, which are hoisted into place by cranes at the building site and joined together.

STEEL SECTION

CLIMBING CRANE

BUILDING STAGES

1 *First, the foundations, piers and anchors of the suspension bridge are built. These will give the bridge a strong, solid base.*

2 *Next, the twin towers are built on top of the piers. These may be made of steel or concrete, and will support the massive cables.*

3 *The two thick steel cables are added, going over the towers and down to the anchors, which are embedded in the river bank.*

4 *The deck is added in sections. Work may begin at the towers and move out, or at the ends and middle and move towards the towers.*

5 *Once the road deck is complete, the road surface is added, preparing the new suspension bridge for cars, trucks and other traffic to use.*

The building process

The various parts of a suspension bridge are always built in the same order. The foundations, piers, and anchors are built first, followed by the towers. When these are completed, the cables are hung over the towers and attached to the anchors. Once the cables are in place, the deck is added piece by piece. While the bridge itself is being built, the **approach roads** are constructed on the river banks.

PULLEY
WIRE HAULING ROPE
STRAND
SAFETY RAIL
SUSPENSION CABLE
TIMBER WALKWAY

The bridge cables are built up strand by strand. This is called spinning. Each strand is put over a pulley, which crosses the bridge on a wire. When the pulley reaches the other side, the strand is taken off, and the pulley returns for a new strand.

Each deck section is hauled into place by tugs on the water, then attached to its hangers. The deck sections are not normally joined up until they are all in position.

CABLES

ASPHALT SURFACE

PAVER

*Once the road deck is in position, it must be covered with **asphalt**. This work is done by machines called pavers.*

TUG

STEP BY STEP

9 The deck is completed, and safety rails, lights, signs and other fittings are all added. Finally the bridge is opened to traffic.

Cable-stayed bridges

Cable-stayed bridges are built in a similar way to suspension bridges, but the deck sections are not hung under a cable strung over the towers, as in a suspension bridge. Instead, each section is supported by its own cable attached to a tower. Cable-stayed bridges are popular for medium-length bridges with a span of between about 200m and 800m.

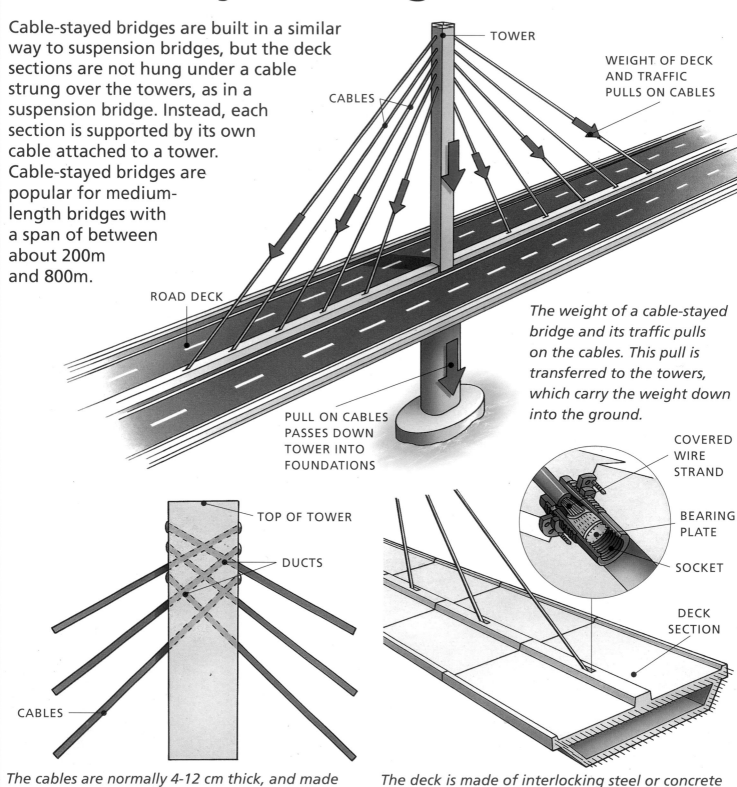

TOWER

CABLES

WEIGHT OF DECK AND TRAFFIC PULLS ON CABLES

ROAD DECK

PULL ON CABLES PASSES DOWN TOWER INTO FOUNDATIONS

The weight of a cable-stayed bridge and its traffic pulls on the cables. This pull is transferred to the towers, which carry the weight down into the ground.

TOP OF TOWER

DUCTS

CABLES

COVERED WIRE STRAND

BEARING PLATE

SOCKET

DECK SECTION

*The cables are normally 4-12 cm thick, and made up of many wire strands. They are fed into **ducts** at the top of concrete towers to hold them in place.*

The deck is made of interlocking steel or concrete sections similar to those in suspension bridges. The sections are linked to the cables with strong joints.

Parts of a cable-stayed bridge

A cable-stayed bridge has three main parts. These are the towers (sometimes called the pylons), the deck, and the cables. The towers and the cables in a suspension bridge can be arranged in only one way. But there are many possible arrangements of towers and cables in a cable-stayed bridge. Often the cables are attached to the centre of the deck, but they may also be attached on both sides.

How a cable-stayed bridge works

Each deck section of a cable-stayed bridge pulls downwards like a **pendulum** on its cable. This makes the cables pull down and sideways on the towers, which carry the weight into the ground. The sideways pull on one side of the tower is balanced by the sideways pull on the other. Each deck section leans on whichever neighbouring section is nearer to a tower. This holds the deck together, and means it is not necessary to have strong connections between the sections.

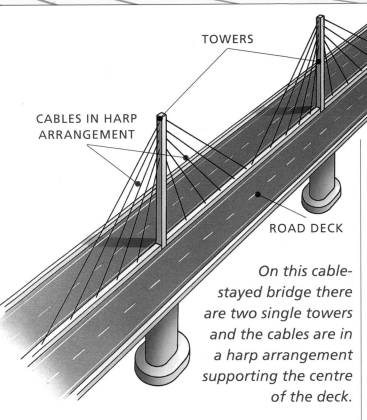

TOWERS

CABLES IN HARP ARRANGEMENT

ROAD DECK

On this cable-stayed bridge there are two single towers and the cables are in a harp arrangement supporting the centre of the deck.

Building a cable-stayed bridge

The building of a cable-stayed bridge begins with the foundations, piers and towers. Then the deck sections are added with their cables, one on each side of a tower at a time, to provide balance.

This cable-stayed bridge has an A-frame tower with twin sets of cables attached to both sides of the deck.

A-FRAME TOWER

ROAD DECK

TWIN SETS OF CABLES

STEP BY STEP

In this space on each double page, we show you a stage in the building of an imaginary cable-stayed bridge. The sequence starts here and ends on page 39.

1 The foundations are built inside caissons that have been sunk to the river bed. Supporting piers are built on top of the foundations.

The first bridges

The first people on Earth were hunter-gatherers, who moved from place to place searching for food. They probably used natural bridges, such as branches or fallen tree trunks, to help them cross rivers. In about 10 000 BC, people began to farm. Different groups of people settled in different places and began to trade with one another. Routes between settlements were used regularly. This is when simple, permanent bridges were probably first built. To construct them, early people used natural materials such as wood and stone.

Clapper bridges

Wooden beam and cantilever bridges were easy to build, but the wood rotted quickly, and the bridges often had to be repaired. People overcame this problem by making the beams from stone. Some simple stone beam bridges, called clapper bridges, have survived to the present day. But stone has disadvantages, too. It can only be used for short spans, and it is heavy and brittle, making it snap very easily.

Simple suspension bridges like this one use building techniques devised many thousands of years ago. The vines are anchored to trees at each end of the bridge.

Simple suspensions

Simple suspension bridges were probably in use more than 10 000 years ago, making them one of the oldest bridge types. They were built in places where creepers and vines were available to make the basic suspension 'cables'. One early design consisted of two of these cables with logs tied on top to make a walkway.

The Post Bridge over the River Dart in Devon is a typical clapper bridge.

24

Arches and the Empire

The Roman Empire, which lasted from the first century BC to the fifth century AD, might not have been so successful without the arch bridge. The Romans had a huge road network, which allowed troops and communications to travel swiftly through their vast empire. All along this network, they built thousands of arch bridges.

The Romans invented the cofferdam so that they could build bridge piers in rivers. Each dam was made using a ring of wooden stakes that were chained together and driven into the river bed.

Roman building techniques

Most Roman bridges had several arches, with piers standing in the water below. As time went by, the Roman engineers learnt how to build longer arches and narrower piers. They wanted to do this because wide piers blocked too much of a river, making it more likely that the bridge would be washed away if there was a flood. The Romans also developed concrete, which they used to bind stones together.

WOODEN STAKES

CHAINS

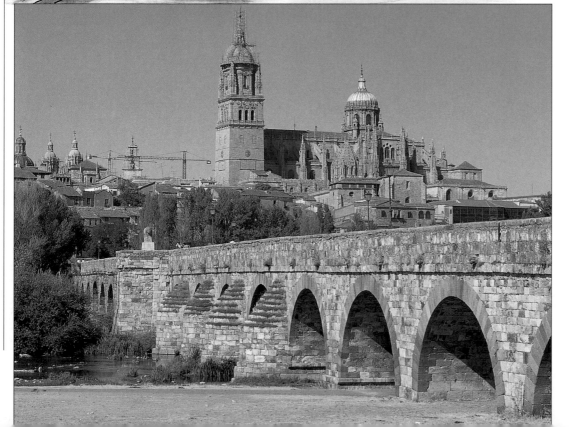

The magnificent stone arch bridge built by the Romans in Salamanca, northern Spain, has survived to this day.

STEP BY STEP

2 Concrete sections for the bridge's road deck are prefabricated in a factory. They are **aerodynamic** to stop the bridge swaying.

Medieval and Renaissance bridges

After the Roman Empire collapsed in about AD 400, Europe went through a period of unrest called the Dark Ages. The bridge-building knowledge of the Romans was lost, and very few new bridges were constructed. Bridge-building did not begin again until after about AD 1000, but even then construction standards were well below those of Roman times.

Medieval bridges, such as the Pont Valentré over the River Lot in France (below), were built with short, semi-circular or pointed arches. Many collapsed because the water flowing through the arches washed away the foundations.

Renaissance arches

During the Renaissance, the revival of learning which began in Europe in the fourteenth century, many advances were made in architecture. Engineers began to understand the science of bridge-building, and learnt to build longer, lower arches. These were much more graceful than the heavy, semi-circular and pointed arches of medieval times. The widest medieval arches were about 10m wide. By the eighteenth century, it was possible to build arches 30m wide and just 4m high.

ARCH SHAPES

Medieval builders used several different shapes for their bridge arches. They borrowed the idea of ribs from cathedral builders of the same time. Ribbed arches were easier to build than flat ones.

1 *Flat semi-circular arch*

2 *Flat pointed arch*

3 *Ribbed semi-circular arch*

The famous Rialto Bridge in Venice, Italy. It has a span of 26m and was completed in 1591.

Masonry arch bridges

Masonry arch bridges, such as the Rialto Bridge in Venice, Italy, consist of blocks of stone or concrete shaped into an arch. An arch only stays up when all the pieces are in place. So as it is being built, the pieces have to be supported. This is done by a temporary wooden arch, called a **centering**. The stones are laid around the centering until the arch is complete. The Chinese were building masonry arches of this type while Europe was still in the Dark Ages.

The Anji Bridge at Zhoa Xian, China, is a masonry arch. It was completed in AD 610 and is still standing today.

BUILDING A STONE ARCH

1 *First, the piers are constructed as supports for the new bridge.*

2 *Next, wooden centering is built between the piers.*

3 *The arch is built stone by stone over the centering.*

4 *Once the arch is complete, the centering is removed.*

5 *Finally, the roadway is added on top of the finished bridge.*

STEP BY STEP

3 The first sections of the bridge's road deck are built on top of the piers. These will provide a base for the bridge towers.

Iron bridges

Iron was the most important engineering material during the **Industrial Revolution**, which started in Europe in the middle of the eighteenth century. New methods of **smelting** large amounts of iron were developed, so iron was soon used in many industries. It was also used for trains, ships, and thousands of road and rail bridges.

Cast iron

One important type of iron used in bridge construction was **cast iron**. Cast iron is brittle, and weaker in tension than in compression. Several cast iron beam bridges collapsed, sometimes because the cast iron was faulty, sometimes because the bridges were weak, as the engineers did not understand how to design them.

Wrought iron

Later, **wrought iron** was developed. It is not brittle in the same way as cast iron, and is much stronger than cast iron in tension. As a result, it made much more reliable beams. But cast iron was still used for bridge columns and arches.

Iron arches

The first iron bridges were arch bridges. Engineers quickly realized that iron could be used instead of masonry to build them. Iron's advantages were that it could be cast into shape, and pieces could easily be joined together with bolts. The iron arches were also lighter than masonry bridges of the same size. So they could carry more traffic without making the bridge collapse.

The world's first iron bridge, at Coalbrookdale, England. It is made of cast iron and was completed in 1779.

The Menai Strait Bridge links Wales with the island of Anglesey. It is a suspension bridge with a truss girder deck, and was completed in 1825 by the brilliant Scottish engineer Thomas Telford.

TRUSS GIRDER DECK

Two of the many types of girder used to make early iron bridges.

TRUSS GIRDER

BOLTS

LATTICE GIRDER

IRON TUBE

The Britannia Bridge carried trains over the Menai Strait inside iron tubes. It was designed by Robert Stephenson, and completed in 1850.

Iron for suspension

The first large suspension bridges had hangers made from iron chains. Cast iron was too brittle to make chains, so wrought iron was used instead. At that time it was impossible to make iron cables, so iron bars were joined together with iron bolts.

Iron beams

Iron is much stronger in tension than stone. This meant that iron could be used to make beams, and that long beam bridges could be built for the first time. Another new technique was to join iron plates and bars with bolts to make **truss girders** and **lattice girders** for bridge construction.

STEP BY STEP

4 The towers are built section by section on top of the piers. They will carry the bridge's weight down to the ground.

Steel and concrete bridges

Almost all modern bridges are made from concrete or steel, or a mixture of both materials. Steel production began in the middle of the nineteenth century, and steel soon replaced iron as a construction material. Steel was added to concrete to make reinforced concrete. Steel and concrete made bridge-building easier, and allowed new forms of bridge to be built.

Steel replaces iron

Steel is an **alloy** made mainly from iron, with a small amount of carbon and other chemicals added to it. It is stronger than cast or wrought iron, but not brittle, and is easy to shape when heated. A way of producing steel cheaply and in large quantities was invented in 1856 by Henry Bessemer, an English engineer. This is called the Bessemer process.

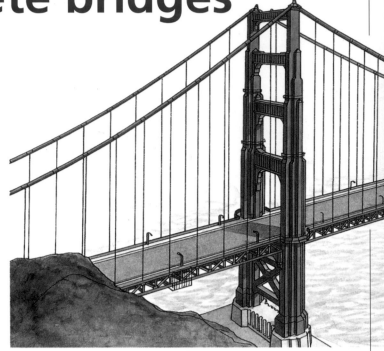

The striking, orange-painted Golden Gate Bridge in San Francisco, USA, opened in 1937. It is a steel suspension bridge with a total length of 1280m. Its massive steel towers are 227m high and each cable weighs more than 7000 tonnes.

The Brooklyn Bridge, in New York, USA, (above) was opened in 1883. It was the first bridge to use steel cables. These contain nearly 2000 km of steel wire.

When the Bayonne Bridge between Newark and Staten Island, USA, (left) was completed in 1931, it was the world's longest bridge. The main span of its giant steel arch measures 503.6m.

Development of concrete

We often think of concrete as a modern material, but it is thousands of years old. Many Roman buildings and arch bridges were built of concrete. The cement in the concrete was made from limestone and a volcanic ash called *pozzolana*. Modern cement produces similar concrete.

Steel trusses and arches

Steel replaced wrought iron for making all sorts of bridges. Girders were made by bolting together steel plates. Trusses were made by bolting together steel struts and ties. Steel arches were made in the same way. Steel's strength meant that these bridges could be longer than ever before.

Reinforced concrete

Concrete is strong in compression but weak in tension. A pure concrete beam is no better than a stone beam. But in the 1860s, N. Joseph Monier, a French inventor, strengthened some concrete by adding iron wires, and so invented reinforced concrete. With reinforced concrete, engineers could build long, low arches, and simple concrete beams.

Steel for suspension

Steel cables were much stronger than iron cables, so much longer suspension bridges could be built. The first bridge with steel cables was the Brooklyn Bridge, which was completed in 1883, and has a 484m main span. It crossed the East River in New York, USA, to join the district of Brooklyn with Manhattan Island. Steel was also used for the hangers and deck of the bridge.

The Plougastel Bridge across the River Elorn in Brittany, north-west France. It consists of three reinforced concrete arches with a total span of 540m, and was completed in 1930. The architect was Eugène Freyssinet.

STEP BY STEP

5 More sections of the deck are put into place on either side of the towers. Cranes lift them from barges in the river.

Towards the future

Most modern bridges are beam, suspension, or cable-stayed bridges made of reinforced concrete or steel. Short arch bridges have been largely replaced by concrete beam bridges, and longer arches by cable-stayed bridges. It is unlikely that new types of bridge will be invented, but new materials and building methods could make future bridges lighter and longer.

New materials

A new type of reinforced concrete, called pre-stressed concrete, was introduced in 1945. Pre-stressed concrete is made by putting stretched steel bars inside concrete beams. This squeezes the concrete, making each beam much slimmer than a normal reinforced concrete beam of the same strength. The steel used in pre-stressed concrete is special **high-tensile steel**. Most modern concrete beam bridges are made with pre-stressed concrete.

The Pont de Normandie over the River Seine at Le Havre, France, was opened in 1995, and is now the longest cable-stayed bridge in the world. Its central span alone measures 856m.

A modern style

Cable-stayed bridges are now popular for medium-length bridges, where spans measuring between about 200m and 800m are required. Longer and longer cable-stayed bridges are being built today. Civil engineers think that they could eventually reach spans of about 1 km.

The Akashi Kaikyo Bridge will form the main part of one road link (1) between the islands of Shikoku and Honshu in Japan. Another road link (2) already exists, and a third (3) is planned.

Better suspension bridges

After the Brooklyn Bridge in New York was completed in 1883, more suspension bridges followed. Spans increased, and decks grew lighter and thinner. In 1940, the Tacoma Narrows suspension bridge in Washington State, USA, collapsed after swaying violently in a strong breeze. As a result, engineers began to build several suspension bridges stiffened by trusses, to make them stable and aerodynamic.

Choice of materials

Civil engineers think the maximum span for a heavy, steel-cabled suspension bridge will be about 4000m. However, by using synthetic fibres and lightweight materials, it may be possible to exceed even this great length in the future.

Building the truss-stiffened Mackinac Straits Bridge in Michigan, USA. The bridge was completed in 1957.

The total span of the Akashi Kaikyo Bridge will be 3910m. The bridge is designed to withstand both earthquakes and strong water currents.

Longer and longer

One extremely long suspension bridge is already under construction. In 1998, the Akashi Kaikyo Bridge, Japan, will open. Its central span will be 1990m long. But an even longer bridge is planned. Engineers hope that in the year 2004 a new bridge will be opened linking Sicily and Italy across the Messina Strait. The Messina Strait Bridge will be the longest suspension bridge in the world, with a 3300m span. It will cost approximately £2.4 billion – almost as much as an undersea tunnel.

STIFFENING TRUSS

STEP BY STEP

6 Each section of the road deck is connected to one of the bridge cables, which in its turn is connected to a tower.

Special bridges

Most modern bridges are quite straightforward to design and build because they are like thousands of other bridges that already exist. But some bridges have to be designed specially – perhaps to let tall ships pass along a river. Some historical bridges look strange to us today because they were built for special reasons, using designs that were never needed again.

Tower Bridge in London was completed in 1894. It has two cantilevers which meet in the centre, but which can lift up to let ships pass. This sort of bridge is called a bascule bridge.

CANTILEVERS

The leaves of a swing bridge rotate to let ships through. The Low-Level Swing Bridge in Seattle, USA, (below) was opened in 1991.

Let me through!

Many bridges are built across rivers and canals. If ships will need to pass under them, engineers must allow enough headroom. Bridges for important roads are normally built on high piers so that there is always enough room, but this is too expensive for minor roads. In these cases, moving bridges are built instead. In their normal positions, these bridges cross a river or canal at low level. But when a tall ship is passing, they can be raised.

CONTROL TOWER

TWIN LEAVES MADE OF CONCRETE

Historical oddities

In the past, engineers have experimented with many different ways of building bridges, some of them extremely odd. The Royal Albert Bridge across the estuary of the River Tamar in Cornwall has two arches made from huge iron tubes. The construction of the bridge began in 1857 and was completed in 1859. The designer was English engineer Isambard Kingdom Brunel. His impressive bridge is still used to carry rail traffic today.

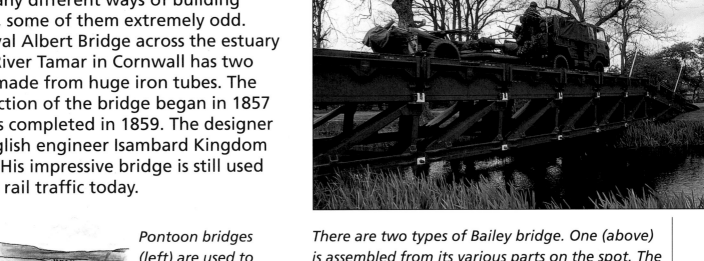

Pontoon bridges (left) are used to cross wide rivers. A pontoon bridge is supported on floats instead of piers.

There are two types of Bailey bridge. One (above) is assembled from its various parts on the spot. The other is carried complete on the back of a truck to where it is needed, then simply unfolded.

IRON TUBES

Military bridges

Military bridges are usually temporary bridges, built to allow troops and supplies to cross rivers. Because of their temporary nature, they need to be light, portable and quick and easy to assemble and dismantle. The two most common types are the Bailey bridge, named after Sir Donald Bailey, who invented it in the Second World War, and the pontoon bridge.

The Royal Albert Bridge in Cornwall has a total span of 563m and towers 67m high. It was opened in 1859 by Prince Albert himself.

STEP BY STEP

7 More sections of the deck are added piece by piece around each tower until the roadway is almost complete.

Viaducts and aqueducts

A **viaduct** is a bridge that crosses a valley. It is made of a long row of arches or beams, supported on piers. Viaducts allow railways and roads to travel over a valley instead of having to go up and down the valley sides. The Romans were the first people to build viaducts, and the name comes from Latin words meaning 'road-carrier'. An aqueduct is a viaduct or bridge that carries a water pipe or a canal. Its name means 'water-carrier'.

BUILDING A MULTI-LEVEL VIADUCT

1 *The first level is built over a wooden centering supported by piers. When it is finished, the sideways forces of the arches cancel each other out, so do not push over the piers.*

2 *The centering is removed and rebuilt at the next level in narrower arch shapes. Then stones are placed over the top in the same way as before. Finally, a third level may be added.*

Roman viaducts and aqueducts

The Romans built arch viaducts to carry roads across narrow valleys. Where a valley was very deep, they built multiple-level viaducts. The spans and arches at each level were narrower than those on the level beneath them. This kept the piers short. Tall piers would have been unstable. The Romans also built many aqueducts, which carried water into Rome and other cities of their massive empire.

The Pont du Gard aqueduct, near Nîmes in the south of France, was built before AD 100. Its three tiers of arches reach a height of 55m.

The extraordinary Lethbridge Viaduct carries rail traffic across the valley of the Oldman River in Alberta, Canada. It is 1.6 km long and 96m high.

Railway viaducts

During the nineteenth century, many thousands of kilometres of railways were built in Europe and the USA. Hundreds of viaducts were needed to keep the new railway networks running on a level. In Europe, most of the new viaducts were built of masonry. In the USA, there were plentiful supplies of wood, and viaducts with wooden piers and wooden truss beams were frequently built.

This modern motorway viaduct carries traffic high over railway yards and the River Tees in the north of England. It is built from steel plate girders and has a total length of 1935m, covering 68 spans.

Bridges for water

Aqueducts are built like road or railway bridges, but instead of a road deck or railway on top, there is a watertight channel. Most aqueducts built to carry canals of the eighteenth and nineteenth century had channels made of iron plates.

Thomas Telford's dramatic Pont-y-Cysyllte aqueduct in Wales carries the Shropshire Union Canal over the River Dee. It was opened in 1805.

Modern viaducts

Modern viaducts are built from concrete or steel beams on top of concrete piers. Long viaducts for roads and railways can be built reasonably cheaply because the beams can be mass-produced in a factory and then assembled on site.

8 The road deck has to be covered with asphalt to prepare it for heavy traffic. This is done by a special paving machine.

Weird and wonderful bridges

During the history of bridge-building, engineers have designed many weird and wonderful bridges that were never built at all. Some were far ahead of their time, while others were simply impossible to construct. Several modern examples of outrageous designs have never been built because of their massive cost. But none of this stops architects and engineers devising plans for extraordinary new bridges, because they know that if they are good enough, they may one day be constructed.

Thomas Telford designed this bridge in 1801 as a replacement for an earlier London Bridge. It was to be made of iron and have a span of nearly 200m – nearly three times as long as the longest iron arch of the time.

Iron London bridge

Many amazing bridges were designed in the eighteenth and nineteenth centuries. At the time, engineers were full of new ideas, but they did not really understand the science of bridge-building. So often they planned spans far greater than were possible with cast or wrought iron. Thomas Telford's design for an iron bridge over the River Thames in London was sound, but he did not have enough money to build it.

*This bridge may one day span the River Thames at Greenwich during a festival to celebrate the **millennium**. The giant, helium-filled balloon bridge was designed by Michael Gold Architects.*

BALLOON WILL BE ABLE TO RISE A SHORT WAY INTO AIR

CABLES

5M-WIDE DECK

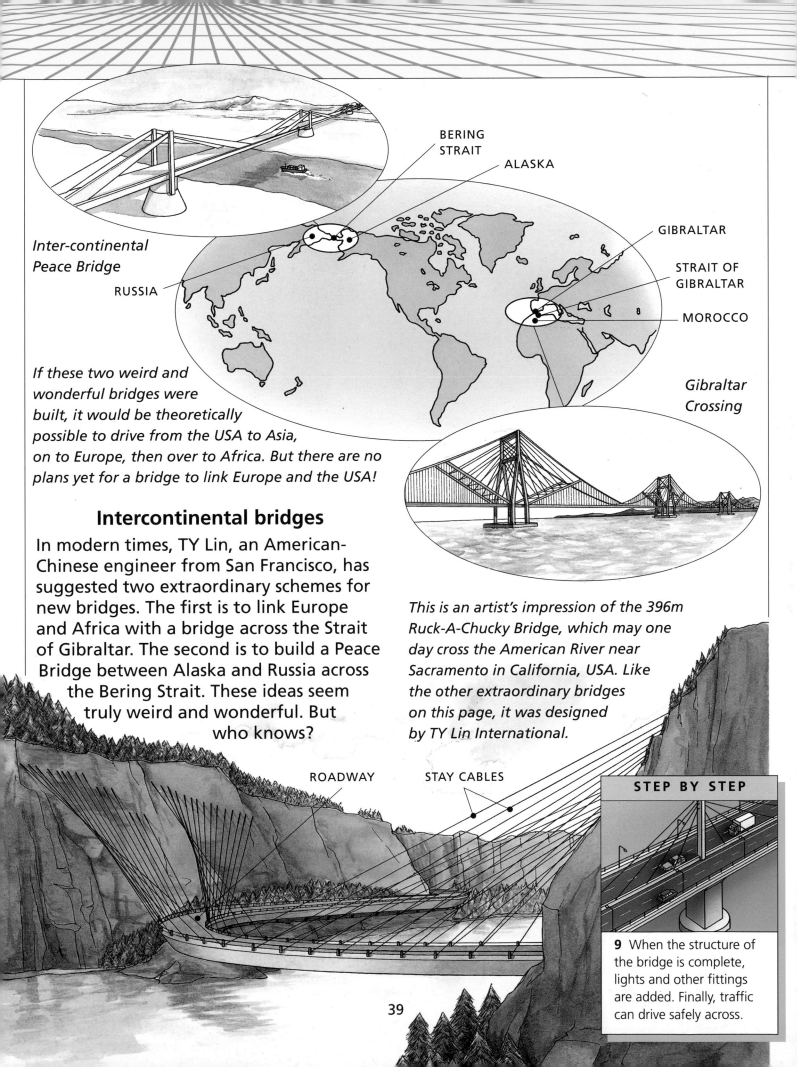

Inter-continental Peace Bridge

BERING STRAIT

ALASKA

GIBRALTAR

STRAIT OF GIBRALTAR

MOROCCO

RUSSIA

If these two weird and wonderful bridges were built, it would be theoretically possible to drive from the USA to Asia, on to Europe, then over to Africa. But there are no plans yet for a bridge to link Europe and the USA!

Gibraltar Crossing

Intercontinental bridges

In modern times, TY Lin, an American-Chinese engineer from San Francisco, has suggested two extraordinary schemes for new bridges. The first is to link Europe and Africa with a bridge across the Strait of Gibraltar. The second is to build a Peace Bridge between Alaska and Russia across the Bering Strait. These ideas seem truly weird and wonderful. But who knows?

This is an artist's impression of the 396m Ruck-A-Chucky Bridge, which may one day cross the American River near Sacramento in California, USA. Like the other extraordinary bridges on this page, it was designed by TY Lin International.

ROADWAY

STAY CABLES

STEP BY STEP

9 When the structure of the bridge is complete, lights and other fittings are added. Finally, traffic can drive safely across.

Bridge facts

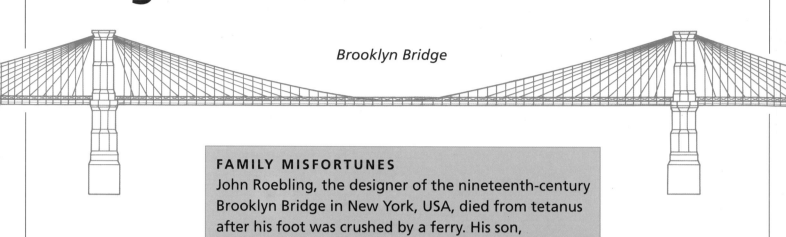

Brooklyn Bridge

FAMILY MISFORTUNES
John Roebling, the designer of the nineteenth-century Brooklyn Bridge in New York, USA, died from tetanus after his foot was crushed by a ferry. His son, Washington, took over, but was paralysed by the bends after working on one of the bridge's caissons.

Chesapeake Bay Bridge

BRIDGE OR TUNNEL?
The Chesapeake Bay Bridge, which links the states of Virginia and Maryland in the USA, is 28 km long in total. It includes 19 km of viaduct, two high-level bridges to allow ships to pass, and two tunnels.

Sydney Harbour Bridge

WORLD'S WIDEST
The Sydney Harbour Bridge, Australia, has the widest deck of any bridge. There are six lanes of traffic, two railway tracks, a cycle track and a footpath.

London Bridge One

London Bridge Two

London Bridge Three

ONE...

The first London Bridge, across the River Thames, was built in 1209. It was covered in houses, shops and taverns.

TWO...

A second bridge replaced the first in 1831. It had five arches compared with the original's nineteen.

THREE

A third London Bridge with only three arches was built in the 1970s. The second bridge was taken apart and rebuilt in Arizona, USA.

LOST LIVES

Eighty-seven lives were lost during the construction of the Quebec Bridge, Canada. In the worst accident, in 1916, the central span fell into the river. The bridge took 18 years to complete.

Quebec Bridge

Time chart

See how bridges have developed over the centuries with this time chart, which shows key bridges around the world and when they were built.

c stands for circa, which means about. It is used before ancient dates that may not be accurate.

10,000 BC
People begin to live in settlements. This is probably when the world's first bridges were built.

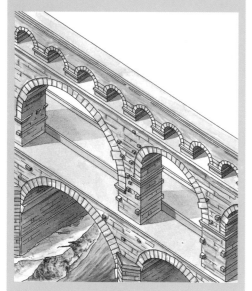

FIRST CENTURY AD
The Romans build the Pont du Gard aqueduct near Nîmes, southern France.

610
The Anji Bridge is built from stone in Zhoa Xian, China. It is one of the first long, low arch bridges in the world.

1591
The Rialto Bridge, Venice, is completed. It is one of the first long, low arch bridges of the European Renaissance.

1779
The first iron bridge in the world is built at Coalbrookdale in Shropshire, England.

1805
Thomas Telford builds the Pont-y-Cysyllte aqueduct, Wales. The canal water is held in a long iron trough.

1825
The Menai Straits Bridge, Wales, opens. It is a suspension bridge with cables made of iron chains. The span is 172m long.

1850
Robert Stephenson completes the Britannia Bridge, Wales, using iron tubes. It is the forerunner of the box girder bridge. The bridge's central span is 140m long.

1879
The cast iron Tay Bridge, Scotland, collapses as a train crosses it in gale-force winds. Seventy-five people are killed.

1883
The Brooklyn Bridge, New York, USA, is completed. It is the first suspension bridge to have steel cables. The bridge's central span is 484m long.

1890
The Forth Rail Bridge, Scotland, is completed. It is the world's first steel bridge. Each middle span is 518m long.

1894
Tower Bridge in London, England, is completed. It is a bascule bridge with two lifting cantilevers which can be raised to let ships pass. The main span is 79m wide.

1917
The Quebec Bridge, Canada, is opened. It is a steel truss cantilever bridge, with a span of 549m.

1932
The Sydney Harbour Bridge, Australia, is completed. It is a huge steel arch with a span of 503m and a 49m-wide roadway.

1937
The Golden Gate Bridge in San Francisco, USA, is opened. Its central span is 1280m long.

1940
The Tacoma Narrows Bridge, USA, collapses after swaying in a strong breeze. It was the world's third longest bridge at the time.

1981
The world's longest suspension bridge, the Humber Bridge, England, is opened. Its overall length is 2220m.

1995
The Pont de Normandie, France, opens. It is the longest cable-stayed bridge in the world, with a central span of 856m.

1998
The Akashi Kaikyo Bridge, Japan, is due to open, linking the islands of Honshu and Shikoku. It will be the world's longest bridge, with a central span of 1990m.

2004
The Messina Strait Bridge between Sicily and Italy may open. It will have a total span of 3300m.

From start to finish

On these two pages, you can follow the Step by Step stories in the bottom right-hand corner of each double page from start to finish.

BUILDING A CONCRETE ROAD BRIDGE

1 Before bridge-building can start, geologists must survey the site. They test the ground by drilling boreholes with a rig.

2 Watertight cofferdams are built in the river bed. These keep the water out while engineers build the bridge's pile foundations.

3 Massive pre-stressed concrete beams for the bridge are manufactured in a factory and later transported to the site.

4 Concrete piers for the new bridge are built on top of the pile foundations that have been driven deep into the river bed.

5 Massive concrete abutments are built on both the river banks to provide strong support for the bridge beams.

6 The concrete side beams are lifted into place by huge cranes working from the river banks. Slowly, the bridge is taking shape.

7 Once the side beams are securely in place, the road deck can be added over them. It is constructed using in-situ concrete.

8 Once the road deck covers the side beams, the central span beams are lifted up from a barge in the river by cranes.

9 The deck is completed, and safety rails, lights, signs and other fittings are all added. Finally the bridge is opened to traffic.

BUILDING A CABLE-STAYED BRIDGE

1 The foundations are built inside caissons that have been sunk to the river bed. Supporting piers are built on top of the foundations.

2 Concrete sections for the bridge's road deck are prefabricated in a factory. They are aerodynamic to stop the bridge swaying.

3 The first sections of the bridge's road deck are built on top of the piers. These will provide a base for the bridge towers.

4 The towers are built section by section on top of the piers. They will carry the bridge's weight down to the ground.

5 More sections of the deck are put into place on either side of the towers. Cranes lift them from barges in the river.

6 Each section of the road deck is connected to one of the bridge cables, which in its turn is connected to a tower.

7 More sections of the deck are added piece by piece around each tower until the roadway is almost complete.

8 The road deck has to be covered with asphalt to prepare it for heavy traffic. This is done by a special paving machine.

9 When the structure of the bridge is complete, lights and other fittings are added. Finally, traffic can drive safely across.

Glossary

abutment A support at the end of a bridge.

aerodynamic Describes a shape which uses the wind to its advantage, for example, to hold it in place.

alloy A metal-like substance made by mixing a metal with other chemicals.

anchor A place where suspension bridge cables are firmly attached to the ground. The anchor can be natural rock or a huge concrete block.

approach road A road which leads to or from a bridge.

asphalt An oily, waterproof substance mixed with small stones to make a road surface.

ballast Heavy material, such as concrete, rock or water, used to weigh down an object.

bedrock Solid rock buried under layers of softer rock or soil.

borehole A hole drilled into the ground to investigate the soil and rocks beneath the surface.

box girder A beam with a cross-section in the shape of a box, made from concrete or by welding together steel plates.

cast iron Iron made into shapes by pouring molten iron into moulds. Cast iron is quite brittle.

centering A wooden arch constructed to support the blocks of an arch bridge until the arch is complete.

cofferdam A temporary circular dam which allows foundation work to be carried out in the dry on a river bed.

compression The squeezing together of a substance. An object that is pressed on both ends is in compression.

detour A route between two places which is longer than the shortest possible route.

dredger A floating machine which removes silt from a river bed. Some dredgers dig with buckets and some suck up silt like a giant vacuum cleaner.

duct A long, narrow hole along which wires or cables are threaded.

formwork A wood or metal mould into which concrete is poured to make a concrete structure.

foundations Parts of the supports of a bridge which spread the weight of the bridge into the ground. Foundations are normally under the ground.

geology *1.* The study of the rocks and how they are formed. *2.* The type of rock or soil at a place and how it is arranged.

hanger A cable or rod on which the road deck of a suspension or arch bridge hangs.

high-tensile steel Steel which has been specially treated to make it much stronger in tension than normal steel.

in-situ concrete Concrete which is moulded on a building site rather than in a factory.

Industrial Revolution The period from about 1750 to about 1850 when industries started to grow in Europe, and roads and railways began to be built.

key The final section to be added to a beam or arch bridge which is built in sections.

lattice girder A steel or iron beam which has a plate girder along its top and bottom edges, linked by a criss-cross pattern of struts and ties.

masonry Stone, brick or concrete.

millennium A thousand year period (the first millennium started in the year AD 1, the second in the year AD 1001), or the change from one millennium to the next.

pendulum A pole or string which has a weight at its bottom end, and can swing freely.

pier A support which holds up a bridge's deck from underneath. Piers support the bridge away from the abutments at its ends.

pile A steel or concrete column reaching down to solid rock under layers of soft soil.

pre-cast concrete Concrete which is formed into its final shape in a factory rather than on the building site where it will be used.

raft A type of foundation consisting of a large slab of concrete, which 'floats' on the ground. A raft is used where piles would be impractical.

road deck The part of a bridge on which the traffic crossing the bridge travels.

silt Sandy particles which are washed down a river. When the river gets wider and slower the particles settle on its bed, making thick layers.

smelting Melting an ore (a rock containing metal) to extract the metal in from it. For example, iron is extracted from iron ore.

span The distance from one support of a bridge to the next. The given span for a bridge is normally for the longest unsupported section (for example, the distance between the towers of a suspension bridge).

strut A part of a truss which gets pushed at both ends (so it is in compression) when the truss has a load on it.

tension The pulling apart of a substance. An object that is pulled at both ends is in tension.

tie A part of a truss which gets pulled at both ends (so it is in tension) when the truss has a load on it.

truss A strong framework of straight sections of metal (called struts and ties) joined together at their ends.

truss girder A truss which acts as a beam in a bridge.

viaduct A long bridge supported by many piers or arches that crosses a wide valley.

weld A way of joining two pieces of metal by adding molten metal between them, or by melting the edges of the pieces of metal so they fuse together.

winch A machine which pulls a rope or cable in order to lift or pull an object.

wrought iron Iron which is much more pure than cast iron, and is better for use in structures because it is less brittle.

Index

Words in **bold** appear in the glossary on pages 46 and 47.